# UNSHAKABLE
# TRUST

A 30-DAY DEVOTIONAL

**NICOLE WESTERN**

*Published by* So It Is Written, LLC
Rochester, MI
**SoItIsWritten.net**

*Unshakable Trust: A 30-Day Devotional*
Copyright © 2025 by Nicole Western

*Edited by:* So It Is Written – www.SoItIsWritten.net

*Formatting:* Ya Ya Ya Creative – YaYaYaCreative@gmail.com

ISBN: 979-8-9912588-5-2

LCCN: 2025901404

PRINTED AND BOUND IN THE UNITED STATES OF AMERICA

# Table of Contents

# Good Shepherd

———◆———

*I am the good shepherd;*
*I know my sheep and my sheep know me.*
–JOHN 10:14

◆ ◆ ◆

When I was given the chance to write a 30-day devotional, I knew it wouldn't be an easy task. This journey has stirred up old wounds and brought to light some of my past struggles. The enemy has tried to pull my attention away through work, home life, and relationships. In those moments, I sought refuge in prayer and worship, though at times, the challenges only seemed to intensify. Still, my Heavenly Father was faithful, always providing me with a word or a sign that He was by my side, strengthening and carrying me through. I am confident that I belong to Him, and nothing can ever separate me from His love.

# Reflection

Write about a time you experienced trials and turned to God. Reflect on how He assured you He was hearing you and with you.

_____

_____

_____

_____

_____

_____

_____

_____

_____

_____

_____

_____

_____

_____

_____

_____

_____

_____

# PRAYER

———◆———

*Thank You, Lord, for being a Good Shepherd—one who knows me intimately and cares for me deeply. You know each of Your sheep by name, and I am grateful for the personal relationship I have with You. Amen.*

———————— ◆ ◆ ◆ ————————

# He Will Act

───◆───

*Commit your way to the Lord, trust Him and He will do this.*
–PSALM 37:5

◆◆◆

L ife has always felt like a continuous rollercoaster of change for me. I used to see my life as a collection of moments where I was merely getting by. But as I drafted this book, something shifted. I came to understand that, despite the challenges and uncertainty, my journey has always been steered by God's unwavering faithfulness. I saw that He has always worked on my behalf, and every experience, even the tough ones, has been a vital part of His bigger plan for me.

# Reflection

Write about a time when you didn't understand a demanding situation you were facing. Reflect on how God brought you through.

_____

_____

_____

_____

_____

_____

_____

_____

_____

_____

_____

_____

_____

_____

_____

_____

# PRAYER

—◆—

*Father God, I know You will provide for all my needs. Everything is in Your hands, and You know my needs even before I speak them. I turn all my concerns over to You. Please grant me the wisdom to manage all the blessings You bestow upon me and to trust in Your perfect timing for all things in my life. Amen.*

◆ ◆ ◆

# Kept Safe

———◆———

*Fear of man will prove to be a snare,*
*but whoever trusts in the LORD is kept safe.*
–PROVERBS 29:25

◆◆◆

Throughout my life, I often struggled with the fear of rejection and failure. I was raised with the belief that stability was key—find a steady job or get married. Yet, in high school, I uncovered my passion for writing poems, short stories, and music. Writing became my refuge, a way to cope with life's challenges. Despite this love, I didn't pursue my creative gifts after high school, concerned about how my parents would react. But now, I've chosen to place my trust in the Lord and am determined not to let fear stand in my way.

# Reflection

Write about a time you worried about what someone else would think. Reflect on what you did to overcome that fear. Then, write a note to God, sharing what's on your heart.

_____

_____

_____

_____

_____

_____

_____

_____

_____

_____

_____

_____

_____

_____

_____

_____

# PRAYER

—◆—

*Father, I come to You today with a humble heart, seeking Your forgiveness for my sins. Please give me the strength to refrain from anything that displeases You. Too often, I allow fear to control me. Your Word says that "fear is of the enemy and not of God." I'm asking You to remove fear from my heart and replace it with boldness and courage like David had when he faced Goliath. In Jesus' name, Amen.*

◆◆◆

# Safe Place

———◆———

*Trust in Him at all times, you people;*
*pour out your hearts to Him, for God is our refuge.*
–PSALM 62:8

◆◆◆

From an early age, my trust in others was broken, and the scars from those deep hurts influenced how I interacted with people and shaped my relationships for many years. I started to associate love with toxic behaviors, creating a cycle of pain and dysfunction that I couldn't break. For a long time, I let my mind lead me instead of my heart. The pain consumed me, spreading like cancer, until I barely recognized myself and desperately needed relief. In that moment of desperation, I called out to God, asking Him to remove the pain and the haunting feelings of betrayal. And in that moment, I found freedom.

Though doubt still tries to creep in from time to time, I have learned to place my trust entirely in Him. He is my refuge and strength, always there to carry me through.

# Reflection

Write about a situation that broke your trust in someone. Reflect on how that situation impacted your emotions, relationships, and sense of self.

_____

_____

_____

_____

_____

_____

_____

_____

_____

_____

_____

_____

_____

_____

_____

_____

# PRAYER

*Heavenly Father, I come before You with a heart burdened by emotional scars — wounds that have shaped my thoughts, feelings, and interactions with others. Lord, You see the pain within me, the memories that linger, and the brokenness I carry. I confess that these scars have sometimes held me back from trusting, loving, and fully living in Your grace. Heal my heart, Lord, and help me to release the pain and surrender it all to You. Amen.*

# Do Not Be Afraid

———◆———

*Do not be afraid of them;*
*the LORD your God himself will fight for you.*
–DEUTERONOMY 3:22

◆ ◆ ◆

In my younger years, I depended on my words and fists to fight my battles. Whenever I felt threatened or attacked, I was quick to respond with harsh words or actions. For a long time, I believed the world was against me and that I had to face everything alone. This belief led me to trust no one and always assume the worst in others.

This mindset created chaos in my relationships with my parents, friends, and even family. Over time, my negative outlook became a growing concern for those around me. A close friend, witnessing the hostility I had developed, chose to distance themselves. That moment was a wake-up call, urging me to look within and realize that change was necessary.

I knew I had to surrender my battles to God and let Him fight for me. It wasn't an instant change—it took a daily decision to trust His promises and lean on His guidance. Letting go of control and fully relying on God was one of the most challenging yet rewarding choices I have ever made.

# Reflection

Write about a time you fought a battle on your own instead of letting God handle it. Reflect on the moment you chose to let God fight for you and why that decision changed your approach to challenges.

_____

_____

_____

_____

_____

_____

_____

_____

_____

_____

_____

_____

_____

# PRAYER

———◆———

*Father, I pray for the strength and will to allow You to fight all my battles. When I am faced with threats or challenges, grant me peace and the wisdom to trust in You. Deliver me, Lord, from the troubles I face today and those that may come in the future. In Jesus' name, Amen.*

———◆◆◆———

# Wait for Him

———◆———

*Blessed are all those who wait for Him.*
–ISAIAH 30:18

◆ ◆ ◆

efore moving to Tennessee, I dreamed of opening a bed and breakfast in Detroit. I invested a lot of time and effort into making it a reality, but it didn't happen at that time. Often, we get ahead of God, believing that the right moment has arrived. I was so determined to make this dream come true, and as time passed, the fear of running out of time consumed me daily. But God works according to His own timing. When He asks us to be still, He invites us to find peace as He prepares us. We must remember that even in those moments of stillness, God is still working on our behalf.

# Reflection

I challenge you to close your eyes and sit in silence for five minutes. Afterward, write down what God said or revealed to you.

_____

_____

_____

_____

_____

_____

_____

_____

_____

_____

_____

_____

_____

_____

_____

_____

_____

_____

_____

_____

_____

_____

_____

_____

_____

_____

_____

_____

_____

_____

_____

_____

# PRAYER

———◆———

*Father, You know my heart and my struggles. You hold my life in Your hands. Teach me to "be still and know that You are God." In Jesus' name. Amen.*

———◆◆◆———

# Wisdom in God's Timing

———◆———

*Be still, and know that I am God. I will be exalted among the*
*nations; I will be exalted in the earth!*
–PSALM 46:10

◆◆◆

From an early age, I valued independence and always found ways to earn money. As early as elementary school, I would save my allowance to buy candy and juice from the penny store to sell. This entrepreneurial drive stayed with me into adulthood, and the desire to own a business, which began in my childhood, still burns within me.

Throughout my adult years, I prayed earnestly, seeking God's guidance on how to make this dream a reality. But God's answer was clear: "No, you are not ready. Be still and know that I am God." At the time, this answer was difficult to accept. But now, looking back, I understand that I wasn't prepared, and I would have failed. Today, I'm closer to my goal than ever, and I see the wisdom in God's perfect timing.

# Reflection

Write about a time you felt ready for something, but God told you to be still. Reflect on what you later learned about why you weren't ready.

_____

_____

_____

_____

_____

_____

_____

_____

_____

_____

_____

_____

_____

_____

_____

_____

_____

_____

_____

_____

_____

_____

_____

_____

_____

_____

_____

_____

_____

_____

# PRAYER

———◆———

*God, grant me the wisdom to recognize when I need to be still and allow You to work in my life. When my plans don't align with Your will, help me to hear Your voice clearly and to trust in Your timing. I know that the safest place is in the center of Your will. Amen.*

———◆◆◆———

# His Plans for You

—◆—

*"For I know the plans I have for you," declares the LORD,*
*"plans to prosper you and not to harm you,*
*plans to give you hope and a future."*
–JEREMIAH 29:11

◆ ◆ ◆

From a youthful age, I've faced countless moments of heartache and disappointment. The pain I carried often turned into anger, driving me to make rash decisions. In hindsight, I realize that some of those choices should have led to far worse outcomes. God protected me from both imprisonment and death. Now, I can say with certainty that I trust Him fully. While I still struggle to fully embody that trust at times, I know I'm a work in progress. His plan for me isn't just about surviving—it's about redemption and transformation.

# Reflection

Write about a time in your life when you made a bad choice. Reflect on how God's plan helped you overcome that decision. Then, write a gratitude note to God.

_____

_____

_____

_____

_____

_____

_____

_____

_____

_____

_____

_____

_____

_____

_____

_____

_____

# PRAYER

*My Father in Heaven, forgive me for the things I've done, thought, and said that are not pleasing to You. From the depths of my heart, I thank You for Your unfailing love and faithfulness. Help me trust Your plan for my life, even when I don't understand the path. Strengthen my faith and fill me with Your peace, knowing that Your purposes for me are good. In Jesus' name, Amen.*

# Believe in God

———◆———

*Do not let your hearts be troubled.*
*You believe in God; believe also in me.*
–JOHN 14:1

———◆◆◆———

*T*hroughout my life, I have faced numerous trials and challenges. One of the most difficult was becoming a single parent. I can still recall the intense fear I felt when I first learned I was pregnant. Doubts, confusion, and anxiety flooded my mind. In search of comfort and support, I turned to my church community. Still, instead of the compassion I hoped for, I encountered judgment and exclusion.

During that time, my mother became my anchor. She spoke words of encouragement that I knew were inspired by God. She reminded me that God doesn't make mistakes and urged me to "hold your head high." She reassured me, saying, "Your relationship with the Father is strong; don't let others make you feel less than."

The day I gave birth to my son, lying in that hospital bed, I made a sacred promise to God. I placed both my son's life and my own in His hands, saying, "We belong to You; I know Your Son paid it all for us when He gave His life."

# Reflection

Write about a time someone turned their back on you in your time of need. Reflect on how God carried you through that situation. Then, write a note thanking Him for His faithfulness.

_____

_____

_____

_____

_____

_____

_____

_____

_____

_____

_____

_____

_____

_____

_____

# PRAYER

———◆———

*God, I am struggling with feelings of doubt and confusion. Your Word says, "Those who know Your name trust in You, for You, LORD, have never forsaken those who seek You" (Psalm 9:10). I am trusting in You during this season of my life. Carry me through and help me hold on to Your promises. Amen.*

———◆◆◆———

# I Will Never Leave You

*Keep your life free from the love of money, and be content with what you have, for he has said, "I will never leave you nor forsake you."*
–HEBREWS 13:5

Becoming a mother transformed my life in ways I never anticipated. I immediately understood that sacrifice would be a defining part of my journey. I had a clear vision for my future—to own a bed and breakfast and, eventually, multiple properties. However, I also had a child to care for, and chasing that dream would require long hours, substantial financial investment, and unwavering dedication.

I reached a crucial crossroads in my life, torn between fully committing to my dream or being there for my child. I chose to prioritize my son. Looking back, I'm grateful for the lesson in contentment that came from learning to embrace what I had at that moment.

# Reflection

Write about a time you had to choose between money and being content. Reflect on how that choice made you feel.

_____

_____

_____

_____

_____

_____

_____

_____

_____

_____

_____

_____

_____

_____

_____

_____

_____

_____

_____

_____

_____

_____

_____

_____

_____

_____

_____

_____

_____

_____

_____

_____

# PRAYER

———◆———

*Father God, I thank You for everything I have. Teach me to be content without becoming complacent. Help me discern when to move forward and when to stand still. I trust that You are with me, and I rely on Your promise to order my steps. My desire is to remain in Your will at all times. Keep me from chasing after money and guide me instead to pursue Your purpose for my life. Amen.*

———◆◆◆———

# Fear Not Bad News

———— ◆ ————

*They will have no fear of bad news;*
*their hearts are steadfast, trusting in the Lord.*
–PSALM 112:7

◆ ◆ ◆

I n my early adulthood, I became consumed by the need
to predict the future. Every decision I made came with
a backup plan, and I was constantly anxious about potential
shocking news, even when I wasn't making the best choices.
At one point, I found myself obsessing over minor risks, like
parking near a tree and fearing a heavy branch might fall
and damage my car.

It dawned on me that my fear of the unknown had gotten
out of hand. I realized I had to surrender this struggle to
God, remembering the words of the Bible: "For God has not
given us a spirit of fear, but of power and of love and of a
sound mind" (2 Timothy 1:7).

# Reflection

Write about something you feared. Reflect on how fear made you feel. What did you do to overcome it?

_____

_____

_____

_____

_____

_____

_____

_____

_____

_____

_____

_____

_____

_____

# PRAYER

—◆—

*Heavenly Father, help me to not fear the unknown. Fill me with boldness to walk through life with complete trust in You. Whenever fear tries to enter my mind, replace it with Your peace. Thank You for being my refuge and strength. In Jesus' name, Amen.*

◆ ◆ ◆

# He Never Changes

———— ◆ ————

*Jesus Christ is the same yesterday and today and forever.*
–HEBREWS 13:8

◆ ◆ ◆

ecoming a parent transforms you in ways you never expected. Your days and nights are consumed with concern, and my greatest worry was whether life would leave lasting scars on my child that could harden his heart. I often questioned if I could make different decisions to protect him from those wounds. It was my duty to shield him from anything that could hurt him.

It wasn't until later that I realized I hadn't been fully trusting God to be who He has always been: faithful, loving, protective, and constant. In my effort to manage everything myself, I forgot to rely on the One who is always in control.

# Reflection

Write about a time you worried so much that you forgot about God's faithfulness. Reflect on how He brought you through that moment.

_____

_____

_____

_____

_____

_____

_____

_____

_____

_____

_____

_____

_____

_____

_____

_____

_____

_____

_____

_____

_____

_____

_____

_____

_____

_____

_____

_____

_____

_____

_____

_____

# PRAYER

*Father, thank You for Your unchanging faithfulness to me. Reflecting on Your endless love fills my heart with complete joy and peace. Help me to always turn my ear to You in all things and trust in Your perfect plan. Amen.*

# Fear Not

◆

*So do not fear, for I am with you; do not be dismayed,*
*for I am your God. I will strengthen you and help you;*
*I will uphold you with my righteous right hand.*
–ISAIAH 41:10

◆ ◆ ◆

Looking back on my son's strong character, I'm reminded of how, at just three years old, he confidently declared that he would be a preacher when he grew up. His faith was clear from the start. If I ever acted outside of God's will, he would boldly ask, "Mom, did you ask God to forgive you?" Even at that early age, he would lay his little hand on someone and pray for healing, and often, the pain would disappear.

As a mother and a believer, I was filled with fear. I knew that if God had called him to be a preacher, he would inevitably face challenges and trials along the way. I found myself constantly worrying, especially when he wasn't with me. Eventually, I realized that my fear was a sign that I wasn't fully trusting God's plan. I had to remind myself that

God makes no mistakes and would guide my son through whatever he was called to face.

# Reflection

Write about something you are fearful of right now. Reflect on why you feel this way and bring those fears before God.

_____

_____

_____

_____

_____

_____

_____

_____

_____

_____

_____

_____

_____

_____

_____

_____

_____

_____

_____

_____

_____

_____

_____

_____

_____

_____

_____

_____

_____

_____

_____

# PRAYER

———◆———

*Father, I come to You in prayer, asking for Your divine protection. Please send Your angels to guard my loved ones and me. Protect my heart and mind with Your perfect peace. May Your will be done on earth as it is in Heaven. In Jesus' name, Amen.*

◆◆◆

# His Creation

———————◆———————

*Look at the birds of the air; they do not sow or reap or*
*store away in barns, and yet your heavenly Father feeds them.*
*Are you not much more valuable than they?*
*Can any one of you by worrying add a single hour to your life?*
–MATTHEW 6:26-27

———————◆◆◆———————

There was a time in my life when I focused a lot on ensuring my son, and I had everything we needed. I wanted to provide for him in every way, making sure he never lacked anything, whether it was a necessity or a desire. At times, it was hard to see how everything would come together, and I would wonder how our needs would be met.

Over time, I came to understand that God was using those seasons to teach me to trust in His provision. He was helping me grow in my faith, showing me that He would always provide for us, no matter the circumstances. Looking back, I see how God has faithfully shown up in many ways, and through it all, my son and I have never been without.

# Reflection

Write about a time when you didn't know how your needs would be met. Reflect on how God provided for you in that season.

_____

_____

_____

_____

_____

_____

_____

_____

_____

_____

_____

_____

_____

_____

_____

_____

_____

_____

_____

_____

_____

_____

_____

_____

_____

_____

_____

_____

_____

_____

_____

_____

# PRAYER

———◆———

*Father, I pray to draw closer to You and to know You more deeply. Let my heart be rooted in You, always dedicated to Your will. Help me to resist anxious thoughts and keep worry from taking hold of my life. Thank You for always providing for me. Amen.*

◆ ◆ ◆

# His Glory

— ◆ —

*And my God will meet all your needs according to
the riches of his glory in Christ Jesus.*
–PHILIPPIANS 4:19

◆ ◆ ◆

et's be real—many of us have daydreamed about the possibility of sudden wealth, imagining how different life could be without lifting a finger. But for me, the real jackpot came the day I welcomed God into my life.

My journey hasn't been without its challenges, yet I can honestly say I don't look or feel like what I've been through. There was a time when my son and I didn't have a place to truly call our own. Yet, even in those moments, we always had a roof over our heads—a home filled with love. I remember riding my bicycle ten miles each way to work, but through it all, I never felt hopeless. God consistently met our needs, often exceeding what we could have imagined, all in His perfect timing.

# Reflection

Write about one of the hardest times in your life and how God brought you through it with ease. Reflect on how that challenging time strengthened you and shaped you into a better person. Then, write a note praising God for His glory and faithfulness in your life.

_____

_____

_____

_____

_____

_____

_____

_____

_____

_____

_____

_____

_____

# PRAYER

———◆———

*Father, I believe in You to provide all my needs. As Your Word says in Philippians 4:19, "according to Your riches in glory." You are a loving, kind, and merciful Father. I praise and honor You for all that You are in my life now and forevermore. Amen.*

◆ ◆ ◆

# God's Existence

———◆———

*Defines faith as trusting in God's existence and says that this faith is the foundation of our lives as Christians.*
–HEBREWS 11:1-2

◆ ◆ ◆

Have you ever experienced a moment of doubt about God's presence? I certainly have, and it's something I'm not proud of. For me, it occurred when I lost my mother.

She was forty-three when she fully committed her life to God, and she never wavered from that path. Her passing at the age of sixty hit me hard. I struggled to understand why she had to leave when there was still so much life left in her. In that moment of vulnerability, I realized that the enemy was trying to take advantage of my pain.

Even so, I have come to understand that God is real, and He makes no mistakes. The evidence of His existence is clear—not only in the miracles He's worked in my life but also in the beauty and order of creation that surrounds me. Every day, I see His presence in the world around me.

# Reflection

Write about a moment when you questioned whether God was real and why. Then, write a note to God thanking Him for everything He is in your life.

_____

_____

_____

_____

_____

_____

_____

_____

_____

_____

_____

_____

_____

_____

_____

_____

# PRAYER

*Father, Your Word says, "When we feel like we have no strength, You become our strength and carry us through" (Isaiah 46:4). God, I ask You to carry me through when I feel weak. Amen.*

# He is Faithful

———— ◆ ————

*For the word of the Lord is right and true;*
*He is faithful in all He does.*
–PSALM 33:4

———— ◆◆◆ ————

For over twenty years, I've built my career in the multi-family housing industry, collaborating with various companies along the way. A constant throughout this journey has been the buying and selling of apartment communities. These transactions often had the potential to upend my life, especially if the company I was with didn't have a position available for me post-sale. Sometimes, I would only have a couple of months' notice before a sale, often with the added incentive of a bonus if I stayed until the deal was finalized.

Despite the frequent transitions, God has remained steadfast in His faithfulness. His Word assures us that "He is faithful in all He does," and I've witnessed that truth in my own experience. Whether I had a new job lined up after a sale or not, God always provided, ensuring that I never went without.

# Reflection

Write about a time something unexpected caused a hardship. Reflect on how God carried you through it.

_____

_____

_____

_____

_____

_____

_____

_____

_____

_____

_____

_____

_____

_____

_____

# PRAYER

*Father, thank You for Your unwavering love, grace, and mercy in my life. Give me the strength to remain rooted in You, especially in times when I don't know the plan for my future. Help me to trust Your provision and timing always. Amen.*

# Have Life

◆

*The thief comes only to steal and kill and destroy;*
*I have come that they may have life and have it to the full.*
–JOHN 10:10

◆ ◆ ◆

*T*he year before I took a leap of faith, I went through an incredibly difficult season of loss. In a matter of days, I lost my car, a high-paying job, and my home. While I had faced challenges before, this felt entirely different. The weight of it brought overwhelming sadness and self-doubt, especially as a mother. It seemed like everything I had worked so hard for vanished in an instant.

At that moment, I was faced with a decision: either trust God or let the enemy steal my peace, my joy, and my faith. I chose to trust God, though it wasn't easy—there were moments when I nearly broke. But God… He was faithful. He provided for us in every way right when we needed it. We didn't have everything we wanted, but He gave us a safe place to stay, access to transportation, and just enough income to meet our needs.

Amid my fear, I prayed, "It's hard for me to rely on people for my stability," since, at that time, everything my son and I had was being provided by others. God's response was clear and direct: "I AM your foundation. Do not trust in people; trust *in me*!"

# Reflection

Write about a time the enemy tried to steal, kill, or destroy you. Reflect on how God carried you through that situation.

_____

_____

_____

_____

_____

_____

_____

_____

_____

_____

_____

_____

_____

_____

_____

_____

_____

# PRAYER

*God, I thank You for carrying me when I didn't know what my next step would be. You have always supplied my needs at times when it seemed impossible. You are a way maker, miracle worker, and promise keeper, and nothing is greater than You. Amen.*

# Be Strong and Courageous

———◆———

*Have I not commanded you? Be strong and courageous.*
*Do not be afraid, do not be discouraged,*
*for the Lord your God will be with you wherever you go.*
–JOSHUA 1:9

———◆◆◆———

W hen I reflect on my own "Joshua moment," I'm reminded of the leap of faith I took at 39 when I left my home state and moved six hundred miles away, entirely on my own. It meant stepping away from everything I knew and was familiar with. At the time, I didn't have a job secured; I just had a small savings to get by for a short while. Yet, I trusted God completely. His comforting words resonated within me: "Be strong and courageous, for I am with you."

# Reflection

Write down your Joshua moment, where God is commanding you to be strong and courageous. Then, write three things that are stopping you from trusting God's command. I challenge you to compose a note to God telling Him how you will trust Him.

_____

_____

_____

_____

_____

_____

_____

_____

_____

_____

_____

_____

_____

# PRAYER

——◆——

*Father in Heaven, holy is your name; I come to you asking forgiveness for anything I have said, thought, or done against You. Father, I'm opening my heart to You for You to cast out any fear I may hold in my mind, heart, and soul. Replace the fear with faith and hope, to trust in You and the perfect plan You have for my life. In Jesus' name, Amen.*

◆ ◆ ◆

# Perfect Peace

———◆———

*You will keep in perfect peace those whose minds are steadfast,*
*because they trust in you.*
−ISAIAH 26:3

◆◆◆

The day I drove to Tennessee, my entire life fit into my 2004 Oldsmobile Aurora. I had sold most of my furniture and belongings before the move. Once I arrived at my new home, I unpacked my car and quickly realized I had nothing to sleep on. I made a trip to Walmart and bought an air mattress—my only piece of furniture for both sitting and sleeping.

That night, as I lay on the air mattress, I was unexpectedly filled with peace despite having so little at 39 years old. At that moment, I understood that I had everything I needed because my focus was on the Lord. I felt rich—not in material things, but in faith and trust in Him.

# Reflection

Write about a time when you felt peace in a situation where you usually wouldn't. Take a few minutes of silence to reflect on the peace you experienced. Write a note to God thanking Him for your growth and the peace He provides.

_____

_____

_____

_____

_____

_____

_____

_____

_____

_____

_____

_____

_____

# PRAYER

*Father, thank You for the peace I feel even in troubled times. I know it's only through Your grace and mercy that I am carried through the difficulties of life. I love and honor You for being who You are. I trust that all things will work together for Your glory. Amen.*

# Joy and Peace in Believing

———◆———◆———

*May the God of hope fill you with all joy and peace
as you trust in Him, so that you may overflow
with hope by the power of the Holy Spirit.*
−ROMANS 15:13

———◆◆◆———

*A*s I began to settle into my new life in a different state, the enemy began to target my vulnerabilities. I found myself struggling with the decision to leave my son behind as he entered adulthood and started college. I couldn't fathom that God would lead us down such separate paths so soon. My worries for him grew so overwhelming that I started making plans to return home. In the midst of my inner turmoil, God's voice broke through with clarity: "Trust Me to do what's best for My children." At that moment, I asked Him to fill my heart with peace. The peace I received was immediate, and today, I am incredibly grateful that I chose to trust God's plan.

# Reflection

Write down something in your life that is consuming you. What are three steps you can take to overcome it? I challenge you to write God a note, telling Him how you will accept the peace He has promised you.

_____

_____

_____

_____

_____

_____

_____

_____

_____

_____

_____

_____

_____

# PRAYER

———◆———

*Father, help me not to worry about what I cannot change. In times when I cannot find the words to speak, help me to "trust in the Lord with all my heart and not lean on my own understanding." Amen.*

———◆◆◆———

# The Lord is My Strength

─────◆─────

*The Lord is my strength and my shield;*
*in Him my heart trusts, and I am helped;*
*my heart exults, and with my song I give thanks to him.*
–PSALM 28:7

───────────── ◆ ◆ ◆ ─────────────

*W*hen I moved to Tennessee, I came to the realization that I didn't honestly know who I was. I had spent so much of my life focused on being a mother, partner, daughter, and friend that when I found myself alone, I felt adrift. I went through a period that I now refer to as my "rebirth," a time when I had to rediscover who I was without the constant influence of others.

During this season, God revealed a lot about the person I had become. He showed me that I hadn't fully allowed Him to take the lead in my life. I recognized that I had often ignored His guidance, letting others shape my identity instead of seeking it in Him. I knew then that I needed to let go of my defenses and allow God to do His transformative work in me.

# Reflection

Write about a time you depended on people instead of God. Reflect on how God opened your eyes to this and what you did to change.

_____

_____

_____

_____

_____

_____

_____

_____

_____

_____

_____

_____

_____

_____

# PRAYER

———◆———

*Father, I come to You with a humble heart, acknowledging the times I've depended on others instead of You. Help me to trust in Your guidance, protection, and strength in every area within me and my life. Lead me as I continue to grow into the person You created me to be. In Jesus' name, Amen.*

◆ ◆ ◆

# You Have Not Forsaken

*Those who know your name trust in you, for you, Lord, have never forsaken those who seek you.*
–PSALM 9:10

Three months after relocating, I began to feel the weight of financial pressure. When I made the decision to move, I had no job lined up and only a small amount of savings to rely on until I found employment. However, securing a job in my field proved to be more difficult than I had expected. During this time, I grew closer to God than ever before. I surrendered my worries and placed my complete trust in His plan, believing He would provide for me in His perfect time and manner. Just two days later, I received a job offer from the very first company with which I had interviewed.

# Reflection

Write down something you are currently struggling with in your life. What are three reasons you are hesitant to surrender this struggle to God? I challenge you to write a note to God, committing to surrender this struggle to Him.

_____

_____

_____

_____

_____

_____

_____

_____

_____

_____

_____

_____

_____

_____

_____

# PRAYER

———— ◆ ————

*Lord of all, as I come to You in prayer, I ask for forgiveness for the sins I have committed against You. Father, I humbly and submissively pray for the strength to relinquish all my worries and struggles into Your hands. In the name of Your Son, Jesus, Amen.*

———————— ◆ ◆ ◆ ————————

# All Things Work Together for Your Good

*And we know that in all things God works for the good of those who love Him, who have been called according to His purpose.*
–ROMANS 8:28

$B$efore making my big faith move, I was diagnosed with a rare medical condition. A year after moving to Tennessee, my doctor informed me that the medication that had been my lifeline was no longer effective. He gave me a stark choice: surgery or possibly die. Feeling overwhelmed, I immediately called my parents to share the news. Without hesitation, they rushed to be by my side. Soon after my surgery, my father passed away unexpectedly. In the midst of my grief, a profound realization struck me: the surgery I feared was actually a demonstration of God's boundless love, granting me one final chance to spend precious time with my dad.

# Reflection

Write down a situation in your life that you want God to fix. What are three ways this situation could work out for your good? Write a prayer to God, asking Him to work all things together for good in this situation.

I challenge you to write a note to God, committing to trust Him to fix it.

_____

_____

_____

_____

_____

_____

_____

_____

_____

_____

_____

# PRAYER

———◆———

*Father God, please forgive me for the times I have failed to trust You. I surrender everything in me that hinders my trust in Your will for my life. Your Word says, "Commit your way to the Lord; trust in Him, and He will do this." I trust that Your will is perfect and that You are working all things together for my good. I praise and honor Your name, now and forevermore. Amen.*

———◆◆◆———

# God is My Salvation

———————◆———————

*Surely, God is my salvation; I will trust and not be afraid.*
*The LORD, the LORD himself, is my strength and my defense;*
*he has become my salvation.*
–ISAIAH 12:2

————————◆◆◆————————

*A*fter feeling God's prompting me to leave where I lived in Tennessee, I stepped out in faith, choosing to trust Him rather than return to my hometown. I drove two and a half hours away, seeking new opportunities. However, after several hours of searching without success, I didn't lose hope. At a nearby mall, I paused in a bookstore to regroup and began searching for apartments online. The first listing that appeared seemed promising, so I entered the address into my GPS.

Fifteen minutes later, I arrived at the property, where the manager greeted me. During our tour, we discovered that she was the mother of my former manager from Tennessee. She mentioned they were hiring, and I instantly sent her my resume. Within a week, I had secured both an apartment and a new job.

# Reflection

Write about a time when you cast all fears aside and followed God blindly. Reflect on how you felt when everything worked out for your good.

_____

_____

_____

_____

_____

_____

_____

_____

_____

_____

_____

_____

_____

_____

_____

# PRAYER

*Father, I'm coming to You, asking for forgiveness for the things I've done and spoke. I thank You for always being there for me. God, I give all my worries and fears to You. Replace them with strength and trust in You for all the days of my life. Whatever in my life is keeping me from being in Your will, remove it. In the name of Jesus, I pray. Amen.*

# He Hears Us

———— ◆ ————

*This is the confidence we have in approaching God:*
*that if we ask anything according to his will, he hears us.*
–1 JOHN 5:14

———— ◆ ◆ ◆ ————

Two years after moving and settling into my new role, the company I worked for decided to transfer its day-to-day management to an external management firm. Having gone through ownership and management changes before, I knew this could go one of two ways—it could be a positive shift or a major challenge. Unfortunately, it turned out to be the latter. I faced significant difficulties with the new management that tested my patience and self-control. Realizing it was time for a change, I began searching for a new job. Despite attending several interviews, I received no callbacks. In my frustration, I turned to God with complete trust, asking for His guidance and a new opportunity. Just one week later, I was offered a job with a sign-on bonus and a higher salary than my current position.

# Reflection

Write about a time you approached God with confidence, knowing that your request was aligned with His will.

_____

_____

_____

_____

_____

_____

_____

_____

_____

_____

_____

_____

_____

_____

_____

_____

_____

_____

_____

_____

_____

_____

_____

_____

_____

_____

_____

_____

_____

_____

# PRAYER

——◆——

*Father God, I approach You in faith, not in doubt. Help me to know Your will so that I can pray with confidence and ask according to Your plans. Thank You for always hearing me when I call. May Your will be done in my life as it is in Heaven. Amen.*

◆ ◆ ◆

# Trust in The Lord

*Trust in the Lord with all your heart and
lean not on your own understanding.*
–PROVERBS 3:5

When I first moved to Tennessee, I lived in an apartment. After nine years, my desire to live in a single-family home grew stronger, so my search for a rental began. However, an unexpected opportunity to purchase a home came up. While I was open to it, I also felt hesitant. Weeks passed without my partner and I agreeing on the same house, leaving me uncertain about the decision. Then, our real estate agent suggested one final visit. As we drove, I realized she was taking us to a newly built community. Without thinking, I said, "We can't afford this." The agent pulled me aside and gently said, "You need to trust God. You may think this is out of your reach, but now is the time to exercise your faith." Two months later, we moved into our brand-new home, having only paid $100 at closing.

# Reflection

Write about a time you went against your own thoughts and trusted God. Write about how you made the choice to trust in God's plan.

_____

_____

_____

_____

_____

_____

_____

_____

_____

_____

_____

_____

_____

_____

# PRAYER

—◆—

*Father God, I know You will provide all my needs. All things are in Your hands, and You know my needs before I even speak them. I turn all my concerns over to You. Please grant me the wisdom to manage all the blessings You have given me wisely and to trust Your timing in all things in my life. Amen.*

◆ ◆ ◆

# Remembered Forever

◆

*Surely, the righteous will never be shaken;*
*they will be remembered forever.*
–PSALM 112:6

◆ ◆ ◆

*M*y partner received a daunting diagnosis: spinal nerve damage, dangerously close to causing paralysis. The doctor's words were hard to bear—without surgery, he would soon be paralyzed. The expected recovery time was six weeks, but after the surgery, weakness on his left side kept him from returning to work for an entire year. As time passed, discouragement set in, and doubt began to cloud his mind. Worries about finances and the well-being of his family kept him awake at night.

Through it all, my faith remained unshaken because I trusted that God was in control. He hadn't brought us this far just to let us fall. I began praying over him and speaking Scripture into our situation. Though my partner still faces challenges, his trust in God has remained steadfast, and we never went without.

# Reflection

Write about a time you were faced with a situation that could have shaken your faith. Reflect on what you did during that time to keep your heart focused on God. Then, write a note to God, telling Him why your faith will never be shaken again.

_____

_____

_____

_____

_____

_____

_____

_____

_____

_____

_____

_____

_____

_____

_____

_____

_____

_____

_____

_____

_____

_____

_____

_____

_____

_____

_____

_____

_____

_____

_____

# PRAYER

———◆———

*Father in Heaven, when I am faced with tribulations, fill me with faith that's unshakable. I know my life is in Your hands and that You allow all things in my life. Keep me in perfect peace while You grow and mold me into the person You want me to be. Amen*

.

———————— ◆ ◆ ◆ ————————

# Blessed

———————◆———————

*But blessed is the one who trusts in the LORD,*
*whose confidence is in him.*
–JEREMIAH 17:7

◆◆◆

When I moved from Detroit to Tennessee, I had a sharp vision of how I wanted my life to unfold. However, as time passed, I realized that God's plan was quite different from mine. As the saying goes, "If you want to make God laugh, tell Him your plans."

At the time, I dreamed of purchasing land and opening a bed and breakfast. But God had something far beyond what I had envisioned. Slowly, I found myself reaching goals I had never set for myself and experiencing successes I couldn't have imagined.

While my original dream remains in my heart, I have come to trust the path God has laid out for me, knowing His plan is far greater than anything I could have imagined and trusting in His perfect timing.

# Reflection

Write about a goal you set for yourself that hasn't happened yet. Reflect on a goal you've achieved that you never initially planned for. Consider how achieving that unexpected goal has changed your life.

---

_____

_____

_____

_____

_____

_____

_____

_____

_____

_____

_____

_____

# PRAYER

———◆———

*God, I know the goals I set for my life sometimes don't align with the plans You have for me. Your Word says, "When the time is right, I, the Lord, will make it happen" (Isaiah 60:22). Help me to trust Your timing and the path You have laid out for my life. In Jesus' name, Amen .*

◆ ◆ ◆

# Do Not Give Up

———————— ◆ ————————

*Let us not become weary in doing good,*
*for at the proper time we will reap a harvest if we do not give up.*
–GALATIANS 6:9

——————————————— ◆ ◆ ◆ ———————————————

L ooking back on my life, I recognize there were times when I could have easily let bitterness take root due to disappointments and hurt caused by people I loved and trusted. I often prayed, asking God, "Please don't let these disappointments and painful experiences harden my heart." Now, as I reflect, I can see how God worked in my life to keep my heart pure. Even in moments when I responded negatively to demanding situations, my heart was always inclined toward growth instead of resentment.

Rather than focusing on the unfairness of it all, I found myself encouraging others to trust in God's goodness. I also stepped in to support them during their times of need. Today, I can look back with a deep understanding of God's more excellent plan and am genuinely grateful for the lessons learned through the pain.

# Reflection

Write about a time when someone hurt you. Reflect on how you overcame the hurt. Write about how that has made you a better version of you today.

_____

_____

_____

_____

_____

_____

_____

_____

_____

_____

_____

_____

_____

_____

_____

_____

_____

_____

_____

_____

_____

_____

_____

_____

_____

_____

_____

_____

_____

_____

_____

# PRAYER

---◆---

*Father, I thank You for Your unwavering faithfulness to me. Help me to continue turning to You with all matters in my life. Humble me in the areas where I am stubborn and convict my heart when my actions stray from Your Word. Keep my heart aligned with Your will. In Jesus' name, Amen .*

◆ ◆ ◆

# About the Author

———◆———

*N*icole Western finds her greatest joy and fulfillment in empowering and pouring into others. As an author, speaker and agent of change, Nicole understands firsthand the challenges of life and has learned to transform them into steppingstones for ultimate triumph. With a passion for creativity, faith, and personal growth, Nicole is dedicated to inspiring others through her writings, short stories, and narratives—teaching them to see beauty for ashes.

Nicole's commitment to continuous self-improvement began in her adolescence and has only deepened throughout her life. Known for her unwavering support of others, she is intentional about helping people mentally, spiritually and financially, without borders. Her writing journey started in high school, where she won several writing contests for short stories and poems, marking the beginning of her dedication to the craft. Little did she know that the seed planted long ago would spring forth many years later.

In her debut book, *Unshakable Trust: A 30-Day Devotional*, Nicole takes readers on a journey of faith, resilience, self-discovery and transformation. With an authentic blend of memoir and devotional, she offers a candid look at the struggles that shape us, showing how to trust God's timing, plan and purpose—especially when life seems to be falling apart. Through this literary masterpiece, Nicole encourages readers to embrace their challenges and discover the strength and faith that will carry them through life's tumultuous storms.

For booking or speaking engagements, email nwestern50@outlook.com or call 734.335.1083